THE ART

OF

HOUSE
HACKING
101

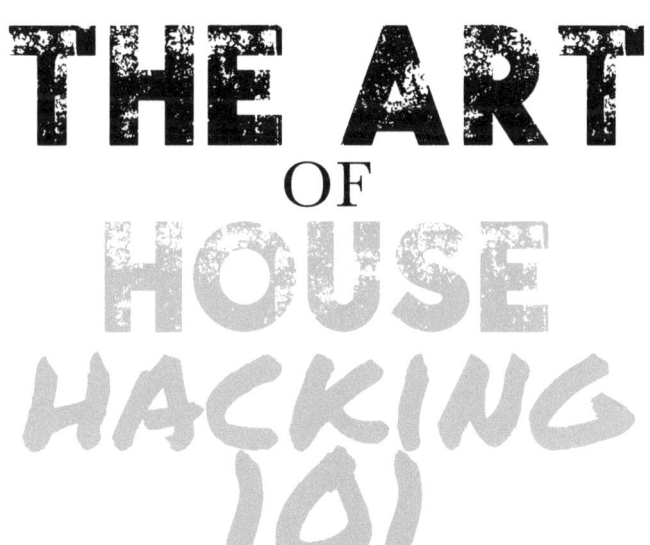

A DIFFERENT PATH TO REAL ESTATE
INVESTING & POSSIBLY LIVING IN
YOUR HOUSE FOR FREE

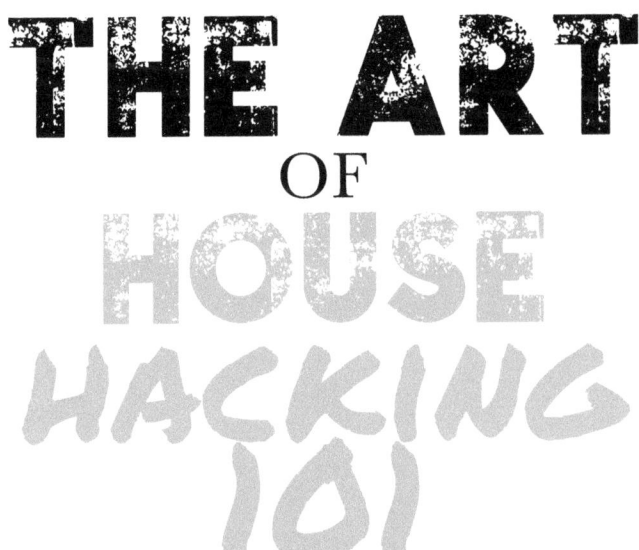

THE ART
OF
HOUSE
HACKING
101

A DIFFERENT PATH TO REAL ESTATE
INVESTING & POSSIBLY LIVING IN
YOUR HOUSE FOR FREE

BALDWIN BALL

TABLE OF CONTENTS

CHAPTER 1

HOUSE HACKING

House hacking was created when homes became too expensive to afford. Many homebuyers choose to rent instead of buy to save money, but astute buyers discovered methods to have their cake and eat it. By purchasing, building, making, or acquiring multi-unit properties, ambitious real estate investors could live where they wanted and have others reimburse the bulk of their charges.

Acquiring multifamily properties, specifically 2, 3, and 4-unit buildings was the simplest way to achieve this. Because they provide numerous spaces to create income and can still be purchased with a minimal down payment, these buildings are frequently employed for house hacking. Even though they have 2, 3, or 4 units, these properties are categorized by lending criteria as "single-family homes."

As soon as people realized this, they began purchasing similar homes, living in one unit while renting out the others. The plan is straightforward:

➺➺ Purchase a multifamily building.
➺➺ Live in one of the units.
➺➺ Lease the others to tenants.

Rent payments from tenants assist in partially (and ultimately fully) defraying the owner's housing costs. This enables the owner to accumulate wealth while residing in the most significant region possible by saving all the money they would otherwise spend on rent or a mortgage.

You can also significantly lower your transportation costs and save money if you can purchase in a downtown area convenient to public transportation or make it simple to bike to work or entertainment.

Most of the triumphant real estate investors I know got their start in House Hacking. Most of these individuals recount accounts of ways they set aside cash by leasing rooms, units, or different pieces of their properties to the people who required someplace to reside and didn't have any desire to pay the whole lease. Whether you're the property holder leasing space, or the inhabitant leasing the space, House Hacking considers the combination and sharing of costs and permits everybody required to set aside cash and work on their financial plan.

CHAPTER 2

IS HOUSE HACKING LEGAL?

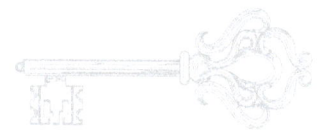

If you don't do house hacking properly, you can have legal issues. Unfortunately, doing it improperly frequently involves disregarding local zoning regulations and attempting to rent out spaces you are not authorized to.

Attempting to rent a garage as a room or residence is one example. Additionally, you can try to convert a single-family home into a multifamily home in an area where it is not allowed. However, house hacking is still completely legal as long as you abide by local zoning regulations and the rental property is up to code.

CHAPTER 3

HOW TO UTILIZE HOUSE HACKING TO YOUR ADVANTAGE

Y ou can't just randomly buy a property and hope to have a successful hacking experience. Before investing, it is essential to evaluate a home's potential. The first factor to consider is the neighborhood's potential to draw a particular type of renter. Generally speaking, you'll have more success renting out rooms or units if the property is adjacent to a densely populated location and is in a nice neighborhood.

Also, consider your budget and the portion of the expenses you are responsible for. For instance, you should ensure that the rent you want is low enough to draw tenants but not too low that you end up footing the majority of the bill for the mortgage and other property costs.

Before making a purchase, you should consider whether a single-family or multifamily home will benefit you more in the long run. The house will be your home for a while, but not indefinitely. Will you be able to find someone else to rent the space you were living in? Or would renting the entire house as a separate unit give you a higher chance of success?

Consider the likelihood of your investment becoming a financial burden when deciding to move out before purchasing it.

CHAPTER 4

HOW LONG DO YOU NEED TO RESIDE IN A HOUSE HACK?

You should take into account your level of comfort when evaluating a house. After all, as an owner/occupant, you are obtaining a loan. That indicates that the lender anticipates you staying there for a while. Usually, if you have a property loan, you must live there for at least a year. However, your ability to relocate while making loan payments may be subject to the lender's more onerous terms and situations.

When you decide to move, that could occasionally mean you need to refinance. As a result, you should always study the loan deal before signing.

CHAPTER 5

HOW TO HACK THE HOUSE AND LIVE FOR FREE

Living rent-free is possible if you are starting your career and are happy to live with roommates. Here's how to do it.

The idea of hacking a house is simple; If you can buy or rent a property with more rooms than you need, you can rent the extra spaces and cover your rent or mortgage. Doing this could mean that she can live in a more excellent area than she would otherwise, or it could simply be a way to reduce her living expenses. Either way, it means she can live in a rent-free property.

As a billionaire real estate investor who started with nothing, I know how important it is to keep costs low early in your career to invest and grow your wealth. If you're OK with living with roommates, this strategy may be for you.

Let's look at various ways to implement a home hacking strategy and the risks and challenges of being a hacker.

While home hacking isn't for everyone, it's a great way to save money for many young professionals.

* HOUSE HACKING: RENT

LET'S SAY YOU WISH TO REDUCE YOUR RENT COSTS. YOU COULD lease a room in a shared home in a less affluent area. But, of course, I would still pay every month, and it wouldn't be the best place to live. But what if you could live in the most excellent part of town, the kind of area everyone wants to live in? Suppose you could live in such a great area with no rent bill? But how is it possible? The answer is home hacking.

First, rent an apartment in the most excellent part of town where the rent per room is high. Perhaps you rent a 3-bedroom apartment, for example. You negotiate a reasonable rent with the owner and get his agreement that you can rent out the other two rooms. Because the area is so popular, it is possible to rent the remaining two rooms for a price that covers the entire rent. This makes the apartment essentially accessible for you. Of course, the tricky part is negotiating the possibility of doing this with the owner. You must show that he will be a great tenant and a working professional. You probably won't find an owner willing to do this immediately. You should keep trying until you find an owner who agrees to this arrangement.

* HOUSE HACKING: BUY

You can buy a residential property where you intend to live in the U.K. with a mortgage of up to 95% if you are a first-time buyer. This means that the main hurdle is not the deposit as long as you qualify. You just need to find a way to cover mortgage payments and other maintenance. The first thing to consider is getting an "interest-only" mortgage. This implies that the principle is not paid; only the interest is. Your payments will be considerably lower if you pay interest. But what if you want to get rid of your mortgage payments? Domestic piracy reemerges at this point.

Suppose you buy a 3-bedroom house with large rooms and the ability to convert the living room into a bedroom. You can then rent three rooms and keep one. If you do this correctly, you should be able to cover the mortgage and some of the upkeep on the property. This means that you essentially live rent-free in the property.

CHAPTER 6

RISKS AND CHALLENGES

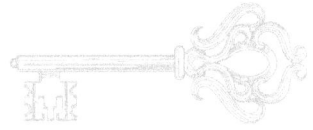

O f course, doing all this comes with several risks and challenges you should consider before taking action. First, you will be responsible for finding tenants if you can't find any of the ones causing problems. You will need to consider null periods when rooms are empty in your calculations. Set aside some money for unexpected periods when you'll need to make payments yourself.

CHAPTER 7

HOUSE HACKING TIPS AND PITFALLS TO AVOID

Want to buy a home but are concerned that the monthly mortgage payment will be too expensive? Then perhaps it's time to engage in a bit of house hacking.

Which is that? When you purchase a building with multiple units, you live in one while renting out the others. You can also turn a single-family house into a multi-family building by adding an in-law apartment, for example, on the top floor and renting it out while you live in the lower half of the structure. Duplexes and other multifamily buildings with multiple units are suitable for house hacking. The objective is to generate enough income from your rent to defray your monthly mortgage payment fully.

Be careful, though: When done correctly, house hacking might assist you in becoming a homeowner. But there are several difficulties faced by landlords as well.

WHAT ARE THE POTENTIAL PITFALLS?

Here are several to avoid.

* LESS-THAN-PRIME NEIGHBORHOODS

NICHOLASVILLE, KENTUCKY'S MORGAN FRANKLIN, AN AGENT with Atlas Trust Real Estate, said she has observed a consistent flow of younger purchasers buying multifamily properties to use the rental revenue to make their monthly mortgage payments.

There are potential challenges, though, Franklin said. Affordable rental properties typically reside in unattractive or undesirable districts, where owners will have a low enough mortgage payment to make house hacking financially viable. These areas may lack the eateries or stores that consumers frequently seek out. They could also have more excellent crime rates.

Franklin said that living in a neighborhood lacking entertainment, dining, or recreational amenities might remove some of the luster hacking that house.

You will enjoy living there, she assured. But, if you are, it will be worthwhile after you are free of a mortgage or rent obligation.

* PROPERTY MANAGEMENT

THEN THERE ARE MATTERS OF BOUNDARIES. YOUR NEIGHBORS will also be your renters if you rent out a place in your house. They might knock on your door at odd hours to beg for plumbing assistance or complain that their apartment isn't warm enough. According to Franklin, proprietors must establish appropriate limits to stop these disturbances. It is usual for your tenants to get in touch with you if their kitchen sink leaks or their water heater breaks. However, you must establish a procedure for complaints that don't need your neighbors banging on your door all day.

This frequently entails selecting a property management company that will address complaints from nearby residents. Then, when they need assistance, your neighbors will just get in touch with this business. The negative? The costs of hiring property management may offset any savings you make by renting out space.

* INSURANCE ISSUES, DOWN PAYMENT DOLLARS, AND INTEREST RATES

FRANKLIN ADVISES BUSINESS OWNERS TO THINK ABOUT insurance concerns. For instance, the cost of insurance for a multifamily house is often higher. If you plan to live on the property, inform your insurance company. Your insurance coverage may be less expensive if you also use the space.

Insurance companies feel that when owners occupy a home, they will take better care of it, lowering the possibility that they will need to make pricey claims for fires, water damage, and other catastrophes. Also, anticipate increased mortgage rates. Franklin said mortgage lenders charge higher interest rates for multifamily properties than single-family residences. However, there is a ray of hope here: You might be required to make a smaller down payment if you let your lender know that you will also be residing in the property.

Franklin said buyers often must come up with a down payment of 15 percent to 25 percent of the property's cost when buying a multifamily property. However, if buyers intend to live in the house, they can be eligible for a loan with a lesser down payment of 3 percent or 3.5 percent if they qualify for a Fannie Home Ready loan.

* DON'T FOLLOW THE RULES? THAT CAN HURT

HACKING INTO HOMES CAN BE LUCRATIVE. BUT IF YOU DON'T do it correctly, it can result in legal issues and fines. And selecting the right property is the first step. To ensure that multifamily homes are permitted in their neighborhoods, owners must first examine their local zoning rules, according to Brad Srutowski, a real estate agent with Hot Properties Real Estate in Norco, California. They cannot hack a house if they are not.

Maybe you converted your garage into a room you can rent out. According to Srutowski, this is typically illegal and may incur sanctions from your local government. As soon as your city learns what you've done, you'll also have to quit renting the space.

And that might only be the beginning of your issues. If your tenants suffer injuries while residing in a compromised space that doesn't adhere to local regulations? Srutowski warned that you could lose a lawsuit quickly.

* BUDGET FOR REPAIRS

REPAIRS CAN BE A CHALLENGE, TOO. INEVITABLY, THE SPACE YOU rent to tenants will go wrong. The refrigerator could malfunction. Maybe there will be a leak in the bathroom sink. You, as the landlord, are in charge of fixing everything. You must therefore set aside money to pay for these repairs. Srutowski advises setting aside at least 10% of monthly rent payments in a savings account that you can use to cover unforeseen maintenance costs. Keep these unexpected expenses in mind, too, when you are calculating your budget. For instance, you might believe that the rent from your tenants will pay your mortgage. However, this might not be the case if you must spend a sizable sum on maintenance each month.

According to Eric Bowlin, people underestimate the cost of maintaining their homes, increasing the expense by two or three when a property has multiple dwellings. Owner of more than 470 rental properties and the founder of IdealREI, both of which are situated in Plano, Texas. Bowlin advises landlords who live in rental properties to set aside 40% of their total rent income for costs. Maintenance, water, sewer, power, insurance, and taxes are all included in this sum.

* CAPITAL IMPROVEMENTS CAN BUST YOUR BUDGET.

BOWLIN SAID THAT OWNERS OFTEN FORGET TO BUDGET FOR significant capital expenditures. They don't set aside money to repair old roofs, replace burst water heaters, or upgrade inefficient HVAC systems. The fact is that the essential goods will all be eliminated at the same time, according to Bowlin. "Since the identical model HVACs were all installed at the same time by the same person, it is likely that they will all fail at the same time. You must set aside money and budget for this certainty."

* HOW MUCH TIME DO YOU HAVE?

THIS WORK ENTAILS ANYTHING FROM INTERVIEWING NEW renters to evicting people who don't pay their rent on time each month. Additionally, it involves appointing a property management business, writing a solid contract, and advertising the home whenever it is vacant. This doesn't imply that breaking into your home is not worthwhile or that it's impossible to pay your mortgage successfully. According to Rotondo, owners that write a clear contract outlining the obligations of both tenants and landlord would benefit. Additionally, according to Rotondo, if you take good care of your property and keep your word, tenants will respect you and are more likely to take good care of your home and pay their rent on time.

CHAPTER 8

SOME OF THE SIGNIFICANT BENEFITS OF HOUSE HACKING INCLUDE:

➤➤ House hacking permits individuals to limit how much capital is restricted in an investment property and is a way for individuals without a large chunk of change to start putting resources into land.

➤➤ Financing the property as a primary residence does typically not require a sizeable down payment and usually provides better loan fees and interest rates.

➤➤ Reducing personal housing costs by using rent money to pay toward the mortgage helps build equity faster.

➤➤ Utilizing charge derivations, for example, the expense of fixes and devaluation cost concerning the property utilized as rental decreases the proprietor's overall gain.

➤➤ House hacking minimizes unproductive travel time and transportation costs going to the rental property because the owner already lives there.

➤➤ Learning the ropes of being a landlord through house hacking is a good first step to becoming a successful real estate investor.

CHAPTER 9

HOW TO FIND THE RIGHT INVESTMENT PROPERTY

* COUPLE SAVING MONEY BY HOUSE HACKING

ANALYZING THE NUMBERS IS ESSENTIAL BEFORE MAKING YOUR first investment property purchase. Carson advises beginning with some elementary math. According to the "1 percent or 2 percent rule," your monthly rent should be greater than or equal to 1 to 2 percent of the total cost of your property.

For instance, your rent should be at least $2,000 per month if you invest $200,000 in a rental property. Otherwise, it may not be an appropriate investment.

Some people set aside 10% of their monthly rent for maintenance, although every house is unique. Good real estate brokers may be able to steer you clear of typical hazards and errors. Hiring someone with home hacking experience makes you less likely to purchase the incorrect property.

"House hacking is excellent for a building with multiple units, such as a quadplex, triplex, or duplex. In a single-family home, you can make it work with roommates, asserts Diego Corzo, an Austin, Texas, realtor and proprietor of the House Hacking Club. Look at similar rentals in the area to determine the potential income from your property. You can look through Craigslist's listings or get advice from your real estate agent.

HOW TO LOOK FOR THE RIGHT MORTGAGE

THE NEXT ACTION IS FINDING OUT WHAT YOU CAN AFFORD AND how to finance it. Finding a mortgage is challenging enough without adding the complication of home hacking.

He hacked a quadplex in his 20s with an FHA loan. You must be able to pay your mortgage at least 75% of the time to be eligible. It's a good general rule of thumb, he argues, but you shouldn't use it in place of a more thorough investigation.

Corzo is in favor of looking for mortgages with small down payments. Conventional financing may be possible using FHA, VA, or 3-5 percent. Every 1-2 years, you may be eligible for another owner-occupied loan. Make sure to benefit from it, he advises. The lower down payment for these loans makes them more appealing than conventional investment properties. Understanding the risks is always essential, regardless of the type of loan. A foreclosure could happen if your mortgage is not paid, which will ruin your credit history for years.

CHAPTER 10

HOW TO DEAL WITH TENANTS

COUPLE UTILIZING HOUSE HACKING PRINCIPLES TO SAVE MONEY

ANOTHER ISSUE OF HOME HACKING IS HAVING TENANTS LIVE with you. An equal exchange of value should take place. Communication is vital after that. The landlord-tenant relationship "can be pleasurable and gratifying if you treat people properly and speak openly," he asserts.

Putting everything in writing might also stop future problems. According to Corzo, every tenant needs to be covered by a lease. He insisted that one of the biggest mistakes he sees is living with friends without a contract or set of house rules. Always perform a credit and background check. Make a security deposit request. He continues, "If they can't afford your apartment, they can't afford to pay a security deposit."

Allen agrees with being firm on the ground rules. Showing you are in charge is crucial, especially if you are younger than your tenants. But, he advises, "Stand your ground and don't let them shove you around."

CHAPTER 11

IS HOUSE HACKING RIGHT FOR YOU?

House hacking is something to think about if real estate investing interests you, but it's not something to get into on a whim. As lovely as a house hack or rental property may be, Carson cautions that entering is simpler than exciting entering is simpler than exiting.

But for the proper person, house hacking has a lot of upside potential. Allen advises trying it out while you're still young, unmarried, and childless. It can be a rare chance to accumulate wealth or achieve financial independence.

CHAPTER 12

10 REASONS WHY YOU SHOULD NOT HOUSE HACK

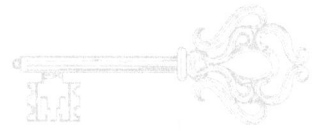

House hacking is the act of investing in real estate, buying a house for a modest down payment, living in one part, and renting out the rest to renters (or roommates) to cover your expenditures. Your living expenses will probably be much decreased or eliminated if you do this.

We regularly discuss the benefits of house hacking, such as living for free, accumulating equity in a home, and tax benefits. However, we seldom ever discuss some of the disadvantages. You can avoid house hacking for the reasons listed below, along with some helpful suggestions.

* THERE'S MORE WORK INVOLVED.

HOUSE HACKING IS ESSENTIALLY A SMALL BUSINESS. WHILE IT IS primarily passive, there are times when you need to do work. For instance, you could have to find a replacement tenant, grant a repair request, or manage rent and security deposits. Daily workload increases, but filing taxes also becomes significantly more challenging. You must complete a Schedule E form in addition to the W-2 you receive in January to save as much cash on taxes as possible. Renting is less effort than house hacking, but most of the labor is done upfront or in the first few months after buying the property. You might add three to five hours a week once your tenants are situated. If you could save hundreds or thousands of dollars, would you be willing to put in three to five hours weekly? You earn hundreds of dollars per hour for the work you do on the house hack.

* IT DOESN'T SCALE

HOUSE HACKING IS ACCEPTED AS A TECHNIQUE TO GET STARTED in real estate or buy your first starter home. Simply put, it won't scale in terms of investments. In addition, some lenders favor lending on homes the borrower does not occupy. Remember that.

Immediately go on and make some real investments if you decide to house hack. Even if you buy a dilapidated house to invest in, you can renovate it to sell it for a profit, but you'll have to pay capital gains tax.

* YOU HAVE TO LIVE WITH OTHERS.

IT GREATLY DEPENDS ON HOW YOU FEEL ABOUT OTHER PEOPLE being present and whether or not you should house hack. You will inevitably lose some privacy. Likely, you can no longer host any sizable parties without first inviting (or asking) your neighbors, even if you don't share an apartment with your tenants.

If you have a family, living among others might be very challenging. Do you desire a stranger to reside in your home with your children? Unfortunately, it only takes one individual to make a minor issue into a major one. You might not want to take that kind of risk.

Living with others can be difficult if you are accustomed to living alone. But living by yourself can be lonely. Therefore, properly vet your tenants if you plan to employ house hacking as a long-term renting strategy to ensure they will pay their rent on time and make respectful roommates.

You will have a rotating door of strangers coming and going from your home every few days if you choose a short-term rental approach, such as renting out your basement or bedroom through a website like Airbnb. It may not sound exciting, but you get to meet interesting people from all around the world. The majority of people are pretty friendly, especially tourists.

* IT WOULD HELP IF YOU KEPT RELATIONSHIPS PROFESSIONAL.

YOU SHOULDN'T HOUSE HACK IF YOU FEAR YOU'LL BECOME overly close to your tenants. This is more of an issue when renting out individual rooms in a single-family home. When you do this, it is unclear whether the individuals you live with are "tenants" or "roommates." They frequently have the feeling of being "roommates," but take care. Getting too close to your tenants could lead to their taking advantage of you, so avoid doing so. If you cannot disengage, it might be a severe emotional weight. When you house hack, remember that your tenants are tenants, not roommates. By getting along and being friendly, you might give them the impression that you are living together, but keep your distance. To avoid this, treat your tenants nicely when you see them, but avoid spending much time with them unless you were friends with them before you started house hacking.

* OWNING YOUR OWN HOME IS NOT ALWAYS ALL IT IS MADE OUT TO BE

THIS IS ESPECIALLY TRUE IF YOU'RE A BIT OF A MINIMALIST, JUST getting started, trying to avoid debt, pursuing financial independence, or enjoying being on the go and traveling.

If this describes you, your unit can end up being useless. It is your fault and may prevent you from completing all the other things you want to do. It can be more beneficial to rent somewhere else while investing in a modest multifamily building for the revenue. House hacking isn't a problem if you do have the appropriate attitude.

* IT COULD ENTAIL RESIDING IN A SUBPAR RENTAL PROPERTY.

WHEN YOU HOUSE HACK, YOUR PRIMARY CONCERN IS THE actual financial impact. Because of this, you can think about purchasing a reasonably priced space so that you can later demand the most outstanding rent feasible. In addition, its condition or location in a less attractive area makes it likely an affordable property. In any case, you will be reducing your lifestyle, perhaps by leaving the downtown area of highrises.

Buying a residence that needs some maintenance is the best way to increase your house hacking income. It will, however, probably be in that less desirable area or require a lot of care. Nevertheless, purchasing a home in need of repair in a respectable neighborhood is a fantastic value-add opportunity. It's "forced appreciation," as we say. It's forced because you increase the property's value instead of relying solely on market growth.

Moreover, there is no requirement that you purchase a run-down home. If you buy that investment without first fixing it up, your cash flow will be smaller, but it will still be far lesser than renting. Choosing your level of assertiveness before buying the residence to hack will be helpful.

* YOU COULD BE PRETENTIOUS IF THE MARKET TANKS.

USUALLY, YOUR FIRST REAL ESTATE PURCHASE WILL BE A HOUSE hack. It's challenging to manage practically all of your savings and invest them in real estate. What if we witness another Great Recession and the market tanks?

It is vital to remember that the market does as it pleases. It is unstoppable and unquestionably hazardous. If the market runs down the day after you close your home, it isn't perfect for you.

Any moment might see the market crash. You must be sure you'll be OK whether the market increases, decreases, or remains stable. Why do you do this? You do the math, then. In any case, whether you have 0% or 100% vacancy, you must be sure you can afford your place. If not, you must ensure that your rent (including a vacancy factor) is far more than your mortgage so that you can still make ends meet even if rentals were to drop by 10% or 20%.

* YOU NEED TO SAVE SOME MONEY FIRST.

YOU'LL SEE THAT BUYING A HOUSE HACK COSTS FAR MORE UP front than renting one when comparing the two options. When renting a place, you usually have to pay the security deposit, the first month's rent, and the last month's rent. If your monthly rent is $1,000 where you reside, you need to budget $3,000 for up-front expenses. You'll need to put between 3 and 5 percent down, pay a few thousand dollars in closing expenses, and then spend additional money fixing it up when you house hack. That "forced appreciation" is what you want, right?

You might put down $15,000 to $20,000 on a $300,000 home. Then, depending on the extent of your rehabilitation, that may increase to close to $30,000. So again, while it's much cheaper than putting 25% down on conventional investment property, it involves more upfront costs than renting. Compared to renting, you need a large chunk of money—$20,000 is not pocket change. Saving money is when you pinch your pennies to get this amount. However, house hacking offers the best return on your investment without requiring you to hire a full-time employee. There is a good chance that if you spend $20,000 on a property, you will recoup the entire amount within the first year through cash flow, loan payoff, and rent savings. Even without accounting for real estate's potential for value or tax advantages, that is a return of 100%.

* YOU WORRY—WHAT IF THE TENANTS DON'T PAY?

THIS IS ABSOLUTELY A RISK. YOU ARE RELYING ON SOMEONE else to give you money to make your investment work continuously. Unfortunately, there will undoubtedly be times when tenants fail to pay. Screening your tenants means you can drastically reduce these missed payments. It is a small price, given the overall return of house hacking. Create a service that automatically deducts rent from your account each month to save you the trouble of chasing down any missed or late payments. Rent can be automatically paid each month by connecting the renters' bank accounts to free services that allow you to put the conditions of your lease on a website.

* LEARN HOW TO RUN THE NUMBERS.

SOME BELIEVE THAT SIMPLY HOUSE-BREAKING A PROPERTY IS AN excellent course of action without considering the precise numbers. Instead, you should perform the same calculations for a house hack as you would for a typical rental property. This would help you put cash flow and possible profit into perspective. Then, rerun the equations for a home hack once you have them in hand. Do it once using the money from the units other than the one you live in as if you were renting out the whole property. You'll get a sense of your cash flow returns from this.

CHAPTER 13

HOW TO EFFECTIVELY HOUSE-HACK A HOUSE

T he main procedures for housebreaking a single-family residence or a modestly sized apartment building are the same:

1. UNDERSTAND FINANCING OPTIONS

THREE POPULAR OPTIONS TO FINANCE A PRIMARY HOUSE through a conventional lender like a bank or credit union are conventional, FHA, and V.A. loans.

Interest rates are often stunning, even for borrowers with lower credit scores, and down payments are maybe 5% or less. V.A. credits supported by the Department of Veterans Affairs permit veteran borrowers to get 100 percent funding on a home.

Before looking for a mortgage, borrowers should, in the words of the Consumer Financial Protection Bureau (CFPB):

➻ Verify their credit history.

➻ Examine how their spending patterns will alter if they get a mortgage.

➻ Plan for additional or altered costs.

➻ Identify the required down payment amount.

➻ Choose the price at which to buy a house.

➻ Make a loan application packet including personal and financial details, such as pay stubs, W-2 forms, copies of most recent tax returns, bank statements, and identification.

2. SEARCH FOR AN EXCELLENT PROPERTY TO HOUSE HACK

A PROPERTY THAT IS A FEASIBLE CANDIDATE FOR HOUSE HACKING may have characteristics that are slightly different from a home in which the owner will live yearly. That is because most house programmers, at last, transform the central living place into an investment property as they develop their investment property portfolio. So, choosing a home that will make an excellent rental right from the start makes sense.

Common factors that real estate investors contemplate when choosing an excellent rental property include:

➻ The neighborhood will influence the type of tenants the home will attract and the rent they can afford to pay.

➻ Property tax rates vary widely from one place to the next and can significantly impact the total return of a rental home.

➻ Occupancy rates and the home's overall worth are influenced by neighborhood quality, crime rates, and school districts, among other factors.

➻ Real estate investors think about the job economy and population growth as two indications to help forecast future demand from renters for rental properties.

- The Housing Price Index (HPI) and the Housing Affordability Index are two additional metrics used by investors to predict the demand for rental homes (HAI). More people may rent rather than buy a property when housing costs are too high.
- Since they will utilize the rental revenue to pay for a portion of the mortgage and other expenses, average rents and growth also impact where to buy a home-to-house hack. Rentometer, Zillow Rent Zestimate, and Zumper are valuable resources for learning about market rents.
- The number of rental homes itemizes and vacancies in the area indicate solid or weak demand for rental property. High vacancy rates may result to lower rents and low-paid investment returns.

3. CALCULATE THE NUMBERS BEFORE MAKING AN OFFER

INVESTORS RUN THE FIGURES TO UNDERSTAND BETTER THE potential income the home may produce before placing an offer on a home-to-house hack. In addition, investors frequently look forward to the day when they may refinance the property and transform the equity into cash to utilize as a down payment for another rental property, even though a home being hacked won't initially be used exclusively as a rental. No matter if the home has never been used as a rental, the RoofstockCloudhouse Rental Calculator is a free tool for calculating the potential return of any single-family home in the United States. Essentially enter the property address and get an expected return figure with basic monetary measurements, including income, cash-on-cash return, rate of return, and gross yield.

4. SHOP FINANCING OPTIONS

PEOPLE OFTEN BELIEVE THAT THE DOWN PAYMENT REQUIREMENTS for real estate investments are the same as those for owner-occupied house purchases, which is one of the most significant real estate investing myths. You have the option to employ owner-occupied mortgages, such as V.A. loans or FHA loans, when you buy a home for yourself. You can close with 3.5 percent down and, in some situations, 0 percent down thanks to these. However, most lenders demand at least a 20 percent to 25 percent down payment when you buy an investment property you don't intend to live in. You can access lending possibilities you might not otherwise have by purchasing a primary house and renting out a room or other units. You now have access to lending choices that most investors do not have. One option is to rent your residence via Airbnb or a similar website for short-term rentals. The most recent tax return, including Schedule E, must be presented. A host report for the most recent year is also required. Income from a long-term renter residing in your primary residence may also be used to qualify for a HomeReady® loan from Fannie Mae.

5. CONSIDER YOUR LIMITATIONS

HOME BUYERS HAVE A CHANCE, THANKS TO HOUSE HACKING. This method does, however, come with certain drawbacks. Not every HOA or regional government is welcoming to home hackers. An HOA or local government can restrict your ability to rent out spots to tenants. Some housing markets also have a low demand. Finding tenants could be problematic with that. Considering house hacking as a life strategy, consider any potential drawbacks specific to your circumstances.

6. CLOSE ESCROW, MOVE IN AND MAKE REPAIRS

DEVELOPING AND FIXING THE AREAS YOU WANT TO RENT OUT before closing on a property is crucial. Although you may be outstanding with an outdated site, the best tenants will be looking for a better room. In addition to the down payment, closing expenses for a primary house typically range from 3 to 5 percent of the loan amount. Costs for origination charges, appraisal fees, house inspections, title searches, lender insurancc, prepaid (such as homeowner's insurance and prepayment interest), and title insurance are among the expenses associated with closing escrow on a home. In the wake of taking title and moving in, they should prepare the piece of the property being leased for an occupant.

The number of repairs and updating required will vary based on whether a bedroom in the home is being rented, the basement is being remodeled into a studio apartment, or extra units in the multifamily property are updated.

7. FIND AND SCREEN TENANTS

THE TENANTS YOU LOCATE WILL DETERMINE HOW WELL YOUR house-hacking plan works. You will just be an ordinary homeowner if there are no renters. Not just any tenant, though, will do. Many inexperienced landlords rush to occupy the space with any applicant. But in the long run, that might be disastrous. With that, it's crucial to screen tenants before moving into your home.

The screening process can be as involved as you want it to be. But you must have some screening to work with tenants who will be a good fit for your space. A few common steps include:

➤➤ Hiring an agency for background checks.
➤➤ Running a credit check.
➤➤ Verifying a potential tenant's income.

You should draft a formal lease once you have located a tenant who passes your screening process. Before the tenants move into your space, ensure the lease is signed. Finding quality tenants is crucial for most real estate investors but also for house hackers. You will be sharing a home with the renters you choose to work with. To avoid problems in the future, you should ensure that you discover a good fit immediately.

CHAPTER 14

HOW TO SCREEN POTENTIAL RENTERS

It's essential to take time during the screening procedure because these tenants will reside near you. Before listing your house up for rent, you should be clear about the criteria your prospective tenant would need to meet. As an owner sharing your property with tenants, you legally are allowed more flexibility regarding what qualifies someone for your property. Unlike traditional rental or multifamily properties, you can be more strict on your rental criteria and more subjective in your decision-making. Perhaps in addition to having them undergo a rigorous background check, you would like them to have excellent references from a previous landlord. Given that you would be sharing a home with your tenants, you might wish to have various requirements for the types of criminal convictions or evictions you're willing to allow.

You can kindly refuse them if you notice any warning signs or if they don't fit your rental requirements. After selecting a smaller pool of potential tenants, you may ask them to tour the property and fill out an application that will provide you with more details about them as tenants.

CHAPTER 15

HOW MUCH MONEY DOES IT REQUIRE TO HOUSE HACK?

The amount of money required to house hack depends on how the home is capitalized and the down payment size unless a fixer-upper is purchased or major upgrading is necessary.

There are several standard options for financing a primary residence to use for house hacking:

* CONVENTIONAL LOAN

A CONVENTIONAL MORTGAGE IS A LOAN NOT INSURED BY THE federal government and may proffer down payments as low as 3% regarding the borrower's personal and financial conditions.

* CONFORMING LOAN

WITH AS LITTLE AS A 3 % DOWN PAYMENT, FANNIE MAE OR Freddie Mac are willing to buy conforming loans.

* V.A. LOAN

V.A. LOANS ARE AVAILABLE TO VETERANS, ACTIVE-DUTY MILITARY members, and surviving spouses and don't need a down payment or mortgage insurance.

CHAPTER 16

COMMON HOUSE HACKING STRATEGIES

T he following are some common strategies people use when looking for a home-to-house hack:

> → Multifamily housing where one unit is the primary residence and the others are rented to tenants
> → Single-family homes with different rooms that you can change into an independent suite by introducing a washroom and kitchenette.
> → Homes with simple spaces to convert to bedrooms, like those with playrooms or dens that can be used as extra bedrooms.
> → Homes with storm cellars, lofts, or carports currently to some extent renovated are a great contender for house hacking.

➻ Property with a considerable part reasonable for building an extra dwelling unit (ADU), an unsupported dwelling like a visitor home or in-regulation unit.

CHAPTER 17

CONS OF HOUSE HACKING

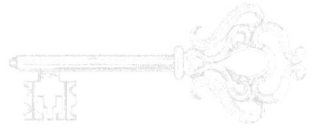

Make sure you are aware of and willing to accept the following drawbacks before purchasing a property-to-house hack.

* YOU HAVE TO BE BOTH LANDLORD AND HOUSEMATE

Renting to a housemate or neighbor creates two distinct yet intertwined relationships. You must impose late fines and file to begin the eviction procedure if they don't pay the rent, cause damage, or in any other way disobey the terms of the lease. However, in day-to-day encounters, your connection is more like that of housemates or neighbors. Who cleans what, noise complaints and scheduling of restroom access are all entirely unrelated to your landlord-tenant relationship? Potential tenants should submit complete rental applications, and you should run tenant screening reports, such as credit, criminal, and eviction reports. Make sure to gather nitty gritty rental applications from all possibilities and run inhabitant screening reports, including credit reports, criminal reports, and ousting reports. Confirm their pay and business, converse with current and previous property managers, and in any case, direct an exhaustive occupant screening. You can likewise protect against them defaulting on the lease and waiting to be expelled. Insurance agencies like Steady will pay you the lease assuming your occupant's default!

Ask them further questions to assess them as a housemate or neighbor. They might be on time with their rent payments, but that doesn't mean they won't annoy you with their sloppy dishes or late-night movie marathons.

* SPEED LIMIT: ONE PROPERTY PER YEAR

When you obtain an owner-occupied mortgage, you consent to remain there for a minimum of one year before leaving. Therefore, you can only use house hacking to purchase one property yearly.

* CREDIT REPORTING LIMITS

Home mortgages for owners For a copy of your credit report, contact the credit bureaus.

If you don't think it poses a problem, keep in mind that most mortgage lenders have a lid on the number of loans you can have. And not a big one either—the typical cap is a maximum of four mortgages. Because of this, house hacking is a fantastic technique to start investing in real estate but is not scalable for long-term real estate investing.

* THE INCONVENIENCE OF MOVING

Another disadvantage is that you must relocate every time you buy a new house to house hack since you have to live there.

Let me tell you: it gets boring relocating every year. Fast. Additionally, it might impact your marriage, kids' schools, and sanity. This leads us to the same idea: home hacking is fantastic for breaking into the real estate market, but only for your first few properties.

* TYING IT TOGETHER

I adore home hacking as a method to live for free and put nearly little money down on your first rental property or properties. However, it is not expandable and has a limited range. Utilize it to increase your savings and accumulate more money for potential rental properties. Loans for an investment property might then be used to expand your portfolio. Nobody requires you to live in a multifamily building if you don't want to. So use your imagination and, if you like, house hack your single-family home!

CHAPTER 18

SOME MORTGAGE TRICKS EVERY HOMEOWNER SHOULD BE AWARE OF.

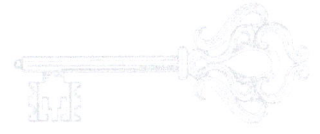

Homeowners may use various mortgage hacks to lower this monthly payment quicker and save thousands of dollars on their mortgage.

* GET RID OF PMI INSURANCE.

Private mortgage insurance, sometimes known as PMI, is insurance that safeguards the lender if you stop making mortgage payments. For example, if you have a traditional loan and put down less than 20% of the home's worth, PMI is necessary.

One method is simply increasing your mortgage payments until you have 20 percent equity. You can then ask your lender to cancel your PMI insurance by contacting them. If you're unsure how much your home is worth, you can always complete an online home appraisal. Refinancing into a different kind of mortgage is an additional choice. For instance, after accumulating sufficient equity, you can refinance an FHA loan into a standard one. Certain new loan types don't call for PMI insurance, even with a minimal down payment. Therefore, if you're fed up with paying PMI, be sure to look into all of your alternatives for perhaps getting rid of it. That might provide you with monthly savings of hundreds of dollars.

* MAKE BI-WEEKLY PAYMENTS INSTEAD OF MONTHLY.

Although most people are accustomed to making monthly mortgage payments in installments, another choice can help you save money and pay off your home even more rapidly. You will receive 26 half-payments annually rather than 12 total charges if you pay bi-weekly instead of monthly. This may shorten the length of your mortgage and prevent you from spending hundreds of dollars in interest.

Furthermore, making bi-weekly payments will help you lower your overall debt, which will make it simpler for you to later qualify for a home equity loan or line of credit.

* REFINANCE TO A SHORTER LOAN TERM.

Refinancing to a shorter loan term can lower the monthly mortgage payment. On the other hand, longer loan terms often entail higher monthly payments, which may seem strange, but in any case, you'll get a good deal on interest over the long haul.

For illustration, suppose you want to restructure your $300,000 mortgage into a new 30-year term. At 4% interest, your monthly mortgage payment would be roughly $1,432, and your total interest payments for the loan would be $214,608. Instead, if you refinanced your $300,000 mortgage to a 20-year term, you would only accrue interest payments of $136,305. So, a 20-year period would result in a higher monthly payment.

* REFINANCE TO A LOWER INTEREST RATE.

Consider refinancing to a lower rate if you're more concerned with making monthly mortgage payments than long-term interest savings. If you cannot lower the interest rate your current lender charges, you may be able to endorse a lower interest rate with another lender. Call the lender and inquire about current rates to see whether it is an option for you if you've lived in your house for a while and accrued equity. You may be able to endorse your mortgage and save money if rates have decreased since you first financed your property. Before making a choice, weigh the costs of refinancing against the money you will save on your monthly payments.

Use a mortgage calculator to determine how much you could save by refinancing.

* GET RID OF ESCROW ACCOUNTS.

Lenders frequently demand escrow accounts to guarantee homeowners have enough cash to cover their mortgage payments, property taxes, and insurance premiums.

Fortunately, there is a method to do away with an escrow account: just plan your budget for taxes and insurance, and then pay the bills yourself. Although it might take a little more work, this will save you a lot of money. Just make sure to maintain your budgeting discipline to avoid missing payments.

* MAKE EXTRA PAYMENTS WHEN YOU CAN.

If you have additional money, such as a bonus at work or a tax refund, think about paying more toward your mortgage. Throughout your loan, even a tiny amount can assist lower your principal balance and save you money on interest.

Before making a further mortgage payment, ensure you have cash on hand since you should always have money in an emergency. You can swiftly pay off your mortgage early if you make enough additional payments over time, in addition to the other strategies on this list.

* PAY ATTENTION TO YOUR LOAN'S AMORTIZATION SCHEDULE.

Amortization is known as spurring out a loan into equal payments over a predetermined length of time. Most mortgages are amortized over 30 years, meaning that the principal and interest are included in each monthly price. The ratio of principal to interest does, however, fluctuate over time. Most mortgage payments during the first few years are used to pay interest. Nevertheless, as the loan balance declines, more of each payment is applied to principal reduction. Pay close attention to your amortization plan and make additional principal payments if you want to reduce your interest costs.

* NEGOTIATE A LOWER INTEREST RATE WITH YOUR LENDER

It's crucial to be proactive and bargain with your lender to receive the best mortgage rate available. Comparing interest rates from several lenders is one method for accomplishing this. You can compel your lender to provide a lower rate by shopping around and obtaining quotations from several providers. Asking for a "float down" option, which enables you to lock in a lower rate should rates drop before your loan closes, is an additional strategy. Even though it could take some time and effort, negotiating a lower interest rate could result in thousands of dollars saved throughout your loan. Even a little rate reduction throughout your loan can save you hundreds of dollars.

* CONSIDER AN ADJUSTABLE-RATE MORTGAGE.

A low introductory interest rate on an adjustable-rate mortgage (ARM) typically lasts for five or seven years (sometimes more.) The rate then changes based on the state of the market after that. Naturally, your payments will go up if rates rise.

However, you'll save money on interest if rates decline. Just make sure you comprehend how ARMs function before enrolling in one. Also, be sure you're OK with the thought of future payment increases.

* LIVE IN YOUR INVESTMENT PROPERTY

A different way to avoid paying off your mortgage is to purchase a home with the potential for investment income. This method, sometimes known as "home hacking," can give you some extra money that you can use to reimburse your mortgage or even live for free. As an illustration, Chad Carson made his first real estate investment by buying a fourplex. He only occupied one apartment personally, renting the other three. As a result, he could cover his mortgage and any unforeseen maintenance costs each month with the money received from his renters. As a result, he was able to live there for nothing at all.

CHAPTER 19

DIFFERENT WAYS TO HOUSE HACK

➤➤ Purchase a home with multiple apartments and reside in one of the vacant ones.

➤➤ Rent out a room in your single-family house

➤➤ Rent out your main residence and live in the guesthouse

➤➤ Rent out all the rooms in your home and live on the couch or in the garage

➤➤ Rent out your place via Airbnb or HomeAway

➤➤ Buy a condo/house for your kid in a college town and let their roommates pay it off

CHAPTER 20

FINAL THOUGHTS

Y ou can save much money for your loan by paying attention to your amortization plan, making additional principal payments, and searching for the best interest rates.

THE GOOD

➻ Your mortgage is paid by someone else.
➻ Over time, you amass a fortune while living for free.
➻ A responsible tenant can enhance your property.
➻ perhaps meet new friends

THE BAD

➻ It could be bothersome to live with your tenants in your house or other multi-unit building (lack of privacy).

➠ Rent arrears and property damage are possible with tenants.

➠ You must take maintenance and vacancy costs into account.

www.ingramcontent.com/pod-product-compliance
Lightning Source LLC
Chambersburg PA
CBHW040857120626
46551CB00001B/61